FANTASY

on 'Easter Hymn'

WILLIAM H. HARRIS

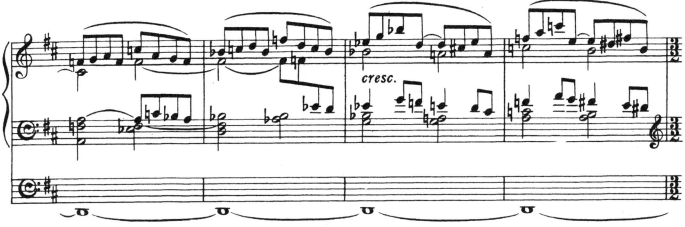

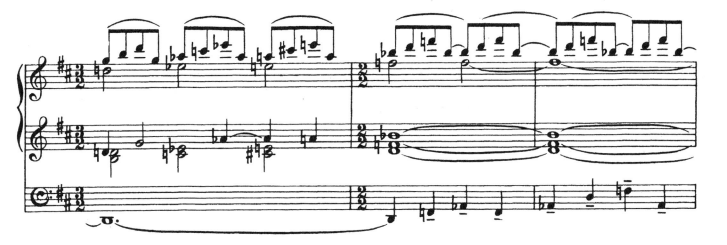

Copyright, 1956, by Novello & Company Limited
© *renewed 1984*

largamente

a tempo (animato)

allarg.

adagio   a tempo

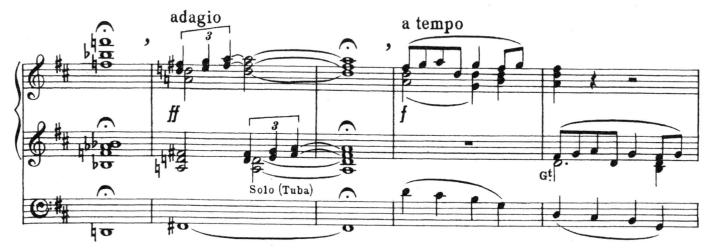

To Healey Willan

CANTICLE

on 'St. Fulbert'

Suggested registration:
Sw. Full
Gt. to Princ.
Ped. 16', 8' & 16' reed
Sw. to Gt.
Gt. to Ped.
Sw. to Ped.

GORDON SLATER

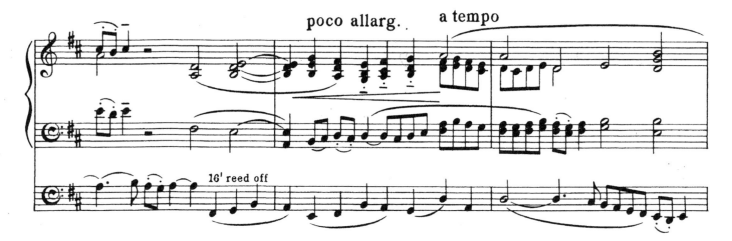

sempre cresc.

Gt to 15th

FESTIVAL PRELUDE

on 'Victory'

C. S. LANG

18252

FLOURISH

on 'Würtemburg'

DESMOND RATCLIFFE

To my dear friend and esteemed colleague, Melville Cook

CHORALE FANTASIE

on 'Lasst uns erfreuen'

Suggested registration:
I, II, III: Foundations 8', 4', 2'
    Mixtures
    Reeds 8', 4'
Pedal: 16', 8', 2', Mixtures
    (coupled to I, II, III)

FLOR PEETERS
Opus 81, No. 2

+16' Gedackt

non troppo legato

poco rall.   a tempo

+16' Gedackt

18254